TEAM ROCKET'S POKÉMON PALS

by Simcha Whitehill

SCHOLASTIC INC.

ISBN 978-1-338-85945-4

10 9 8 7 6 5 4 3 2 1   23 24 25 26 27

Designed by Cheung Tai

Printed in China   68

First Printing 2023

Contents

INTRODUCING...
TEAM ROCKET!

Jessie, James, and Meowth are members of Team Rocket. Together, they have created countless outrageous plans to steal as many Pokémon as possible, but luckily someone is always there to stop them—that someone is Ash! With the help of his friends, or "the twerps," as Team Rocket likes to call them, Ash has put an end to their schemes, which mostly involve poaching his best friend, Pikachu.

Despite their focus on other people's Pokémon, Jessie and James have actually created a deep bond with many of their own Pokémon partners. These loyal friends have proudly stood by Team Rocket through the good times and the blasting-off times. So, it's no wonder some have even reduced these too-cool villains to tears when they have to part. As it turns out, Team Rocket has a heart!

In this book, you'll learn all about some of the Pokémon that Team Rocket has loved and sometimes even lost along the way. But first, let's get to know the members of Team Rocket!

GIOVANNI: THE BOSS

Giovanni likes to be dressed in a sharp suit and have his Pokémon pal Persian by his side. At one time, he was even the gym leader of Viridian City, but now he focuses solely on Team Rocket. To Jessie, James, and Meowth, he's known as the "Boss," and they are always trying to please him. Their main goal is to catch strong Pokémon and give them to Giovanni.

They desperately want to impress Giovanni and be seen as important members of the Team Rocket organization. They believe catching Ash's pal Pikachu is the ticket to being the Boss's favorite, and they have become obsessed with it.

Giovanni has one main rule when it comes to the Pokémon that Team Rocket can travel with—they are not allowed to have any Pokémon on hand that are unusual for the region they're visiting. He does not want them attracting any unnecessary attention when they're on their secret assignments. So, often, Jessie, James, and Meowth have either left their Pokémon with the Boss or back in their home region. They are very dedicated to their work as Team Rocket.

Although Jessie, James, and Meowth usually fumble their missions, Giovanni still provides them with many of the tools they would need to succeed. In the Galar region, he even sends them a special Pelipper messenger that brings them Pokémon to battle with when they need it. What service!

PERSIAN
The Classy Cat Pokémon

Height: 3'03"
Weight: 70.5 lbs.
Type: Normal

IMPRESSIVE SKILLS:
It's pretty hard to impress Persian. You might be able to win it over eventually, but if you ever make it mad, the claws will come out!

FUN FACTS:

- Giovanni's pal Persian is known to sit by his side or even in his lap at headquarters, but in a Team Rocket operation, it is hardly there just to be pet by the Boss. During a mission to capture the Mythical Pokémon Meloetta, Giovanni calls on Persian to trap Ash and Pikachu in a cage; it succeeds and Meloetta is forced to go with the Boss to protect its pals.

- Persian is beloved by the Boss and that makes Meowth extremely jealous, especially since it's the evolved form of Meowth. In fact, when Mismagius sends it into a dream state, Meowth imagines that the Boss tosses Persian and asks Meowth to stay by his side. A Meowth can dream, can't it?

MEOWTH
The Scratch Cat Pokémon

Height: 1'04"
Weight: 9.3 lbs.
Type: Normal

IMPRESSIVE SKILLS:
It loves to collect shiny things. If it's in a good mood, it might even let its Trainer have a look at its hoard of treasures.

FUN FACTS:

- Amazingly enough, Meowth of Team Rocket fame is the rare Pokémon that can communicate with humans and speak their language. It is not a power wasted on this hilarious Pokémon pal! Meowth is known for its snappy one-liners and it likes to inject "Meowth, that's right!" at the end of the classic Team Rocket motto. Amazingly enough, the first human word Meowth understood was "rocket." Clearly, it was destined to join the Team.

- After its first battle with the twerps, Pikachu blasts off Team Rocket. Meowth is so taken by Pikachu's impressive blast that it becomes obsessed with the idea of purloining Ash's powerful pal. And the rest is history . . .

- Team Rocket isn't the first gang Meowth joins. As a young Meowth, its first memory is of being alone and hungry. After Meowth sees its first movie, where another Meowth eats ice cream and fried chicken, Meowth decides to go to Hollywood to find a better life. In Hollywood, it finds a powerful Persian leading a pack of wild Meowth. They offer it scraps to eat, and it is so happy, it joins their street gang.

- Although Meowth finds a way to get food, it is still missing love. One day in Hollywood, Meowth spots a pampered, pretty female Meowth named Meowzie in the window of a shop and falls for her instantly. It tries to impress her, but Meowzie wants nothing to do with rough-and-tumble Meowth. She says Meowth could never treat her as good and well as her Trainer, who keeps Meowzie in a diamond-studded Poké Ball. Meowth refuses to give up and decides to become like a human to win Meowzie's love. Meowth trains hard to learn to walk on two legs like a person and to talk like a person, too, but when it returns to its beloved Meowzie, walking and talking with a bouquet of flowers in hand, she rejects Meowth. Heartbroken, Meowth joins Team Rocket to find its fortune. Later, when Meowth returns to Hollywood, it finds Meowzie living with the very street gang it once did. With the help of its Team Rocket pals, it challenges the pack leader, Persian, to a battle to rescue Meowzie. Although Meowth wins the battle, Meowzie chooses to stay with Persian. If that wasn't bad enough, she adds that she would never be with Meowth. But with Jessie and James by its side, Meowth realizes it might not have found love, but it does have a true bond of friendship with its Team Rocket pals.

- Team Rocket's infamous ride, a hot air balloon, is in the shape of Meowth's head. If that's not love, what is?

- Meowth thinks it strikes luck when it accidentally lands on an island where the locals worship Meowth. They believe Meowth's arrival means their prophecy has come true and it is the "Meowth of Bounty" they have been waiting for. Meowth loves being worshiped on a throne and given free food and entertainment, of course. So, when Jessie and James wash up on the shore soon after, it has its old pals thrown off the island before they can blow its cover and ruin its free ride. However, Meowth soon finds there is no such thing as a free lunch! The locals demand Meowth use Pay Day, a move that gifts coins, to make the islanders rich. This is a special attack Meowth does not know, but the islanders insist it just needs a battle challenge to bring it out. So, they pit Meowth in an arena against mighty Nidoking and giant Onix. Thankfully, Jessie and James are still spying on their pal and decide to help it out. Jessie tosses all their coins and James even throws his beloved bottle caps onto the battlefield. Their trick works and the islanders think Meowth has blessed them with this money. Confused as to where the coins come from, Meowth soon spots a bottle cap in the mix and knows its Team Rocket pals rescued it. Meowth is so touched, it gives up its special spot as the spoiled ruler of the island to rejoin Team Rocket. After all, real friends are priceless!

● While dining out at a ramen restaurant, Jessie and James run into an old friend from their Team Rocket training school days—Christopher. Although he isn't much of a goon, he's made quite a name for himself as the owner of this chain of noodle shops. When Christopher sees Meowth chowing down, he realizes it has the perfect claws to become a noodle-making master and offers Meowth a job. At Christopher's restaurant, Meowth quickly finds success as a cool chef. However, when he hears Jessie and James are in trouble with a special silver Metagross, it returns to Team Rocket to help its friends.

● When Ash and his pals find Meowth frail and alone, they nurse their enemy back to health. Meowth tells them it is no longer a part of Team Rocket because it was fired by the Boss for messing up a mission in the Unova region. Since it is too weak to go on by itself, the twerps generously offer to take Meowth along with them. Meowth bravely helps them rescue Axew and save a wild Scrafty from Mandibuzz. Ash's pal Iris is so impressed, she even tries to catch it, but Meowth doesn't want a Trainer. While Meowth travels with Ash and his pals, it does a lot of do-gooding. Meowth helps reunite Purrloin and its Trainer, battles back Beheeyem, negotiates peace for two packs of Beartic, and brings Cubchoo back together. Though not everything is what it seems. When Ash and his pals arrive in Nimbasa City, Meowth takes the twerps' Pokémon pals for a special massage, but it is really using them for access to the Pokémon Center Vault, where it plans to steal the Pokémon there! Luckily, Ash brings Team Rocket's evil plan to an end, but Ash admits he really liked traveling with Meowth. Who wouldn't?

When Galar Particles are sent flying through the region, Team Rocket's pal Meowth Gigantamaxes for the first time. Jessie and James are able to convince it to turn its newfound energy to battle back Eternatus and Chairman Rose's evil plan. Meowth manages to start its G-Move, Gold Rush, but it is no match for the powerful Legendary Pokémon and is soon snapped back down to its regular size. Then Meowth and its Team Rocket pals are sent blasting off, of course, by Eternatus.

JESSIE

Who is the most clever member of Team Rocket? Jessie would say it is definitely her! Who is the most important member of Team Rocket? Why, Jessie will tell you it's absolutely her! Who is the most beautiful member of Team Rocket? Clearly, Jessie would say it is Jessie! She is very impressed by her gorgeous appearance and takes especially good care of her fabulous magenta hair. Although she loves no one more than her selfish self, she has certainly adored her Pokémon pals. She loves to step onto a stage and show off both her charm and Pokémon by competing in Pokémon Showcases and Contests. While not all of her performances are well received, Jessie never lets anyone else's opinion faze her. After all, she's the one, the only, amazing Jessie!

WOBBUFFET
The Patient Pokémon

Height: 4'03"
Weight: 62.8 lbs.
Type: Psychic

IMPRESSIVE SKILLS:

Wobbuffet is not really the ideal Pokémon for an aggressive villain. It never ever strikes first and prefers to stay hidden in darkness. If it is attacked, it will puff up its body to build up its response.

FUN FACTS:

Wobbuffet's original Trainer was a boy named Benny. He went to a Pokémon swap meet because he was desperate to trade it for another Pokémon pal. Fortunately for Benny, Jessie was there in the wrong place at the wrong time and accidentally dropped her Lickitung pal's Poké Ball into the trade machine. She didn't realize her mistake until she called on Lickitung to battle back Ash and his pals and out came Wobbuffet. Surprise!

- Jessie's pal Wobbuffet likes to burst out of its Poké Ball and loudly announce itself. It especially likes to get the last word in the Team Rocket motto: Wobbuffet!

- When Team Rocket releases Claydol from a giant Poké Ball relic, locals fear it will destroy their small village. As local legend has it, only a fair maiden can distract Claydol long enough to be captured. Jessie, Ash's pal May, and Meowth all try their best to get Claydol's attention, but it only has eyes for Wobbuffet. Claydol instantly falls for the blue babe. While this shocks even its Team Rocket pals, Wobbuffet's allure works to lure Claydol, and it is successfully recaptured.

- Wobbuffet, too, falls in love, but with a party-loving Kirlia that can really dance. With blushing cheeks, romantic Wobbuffet hands Kirlia a beautiful flower. Meanwhile, the local Ghost-type Pokémon team up with Jessie, James, and Meowth to try to stop their party and catch them. They arrive disguised as a gigantic fake Haunter. Wobbuffet won't let anything happen to its beloved and even jumps into that fake Haunter's mouth. Soon, that Haunter is revealed to be just another Team Rocket mecha disguised by the Ghost-type. Loyal to its sweet Kirlia, Wobbuffet battles back its own Trainer and friends and breaks Team Rocket's mecha, as well as the cage that held Kirlia and Pikachu. Unfortunately for Wobbuffet, it ultimately blasts off with the rest of Team Rocket and leaves a heartbroken Kirlia behind. Sigh, it's better to have loved and lost than to never have loved at all!

- Since the Boss has a strict policy that Team Rocket members cannot draw attention to themselves with Pokémon that are unusual to a specific region, Wobbuffet and Jessie were forced to part ways as Team Rocket traveled to Unova. But thankfully, the pair reunited to travel together again through Kalos, Alola, and Galar and have been inseparable ever since!

GOURGEIST
The Pumpkin Pokémon

Height: 2'11"

Weight: 27.6 lbs.

Type: Ghost-Grass

IMPRESSIVE SKILLS:

If you hear a knock at your door on the night of a new moon, don't answer it! Gourgeist will take anyone who greets it off to the afterlife.

FUN FACTS:

- Jessie's friendship with Pumpkaboo was groundbreaking, literally. While running away from an angry Pangoro in the forest, Jessie trips over a Pokémon who was sleeping peacefully underground—Pumpkaboo. As it rises up out of the dirt, all aglow, Jessie thinks fast and tosses her Poké Ball to catch it. The two have been together ever since!

- When Jessie's precious pal Pumpkaboo catches the eye of a certain Prince Pumpkaboo, its Trainer the Count invites them to visit his castle. The Count is quite taken with Pumpkaboo, as it is the largest female one he has seen and proposes a trade—his Mawile in exchange for Pumpkaboo. At first, Jessie is heartsick at the thought of losing her pal, but eventually gets excited when she learns Mawile can Mega Evolve. Now that the deal is set, the two Trainers put their Poké Balls in the training machine, but Pumpkaboo becomes so angry with Jessie that it evolves into Gourgeist. Prince Pumpkaboo is no longer interested and the trade is reversed leaving Jessie and Gourgeist happily reunited.

ARBOK
The Cobra Pokémon

Height: 11' 06"
Weight: 143.3 lbs.
Type: Poison

IMPRESSIVE SKILLS:
Scientists have found six different variations of design on Arbok's body. But don't get too caught up admiring its beautiful artwork or you might find yourself under attack.

FUN FACTS:

- Friendship truly is a gift, and for Jessie, it was a birthday gift. She was given Ekans's Poké Ball as the perfect present.

- Jessie and James hope to force their Pokémon pals, Ekans and Koffing, to evolve with the "Principle of Induced Evolution" but when they realize that principle means hard work and experience, they give up, of course. They soon remember that they love their Pokémon just the way they are. As a show of love to their Trainers, Ekans evolves into Arbok at the same time as James's pal Koffing evolves into Weezing.

- When Team Rocket encounters a cage full of Ekans in the woods, Jessie commands Arbok to strike. Arbok refuses, as it can tell the Ekans are already hurt enough. Team Rocket decides they want to free the Pokémon, if only to catch them all for themselves. However, when they come face-to-face with the evil Pokémon poacher Rico in battle, they realize the right thing to do is to set all the Ekans and Koffing free, and to release Arbok and Weezing to follow and protect them. At first, Arbok and Weezing don't want to leave their beloved Trainers. They cry out watching Jessie and James fight Rico and Tyranitar themselves. However, Arbok knows these poor Ekans and Koffing really do need their help and accepts Jessie's selflessness. Although rare, it goes to show that Team Rocket isn't all bad—they do have hearts of gold, too.

SEVIPER
The Fang Snake Pokémon

Height: 8'10"
Weight: 115.7 lbs.
Type: Poison

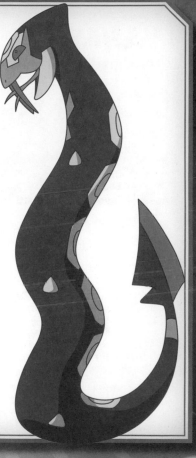

IMPRESSIVE SKILLS:

When Seviper uses its sword-shaped tail to slash a foe, it also delivers a special poison.

FUN FACTS:

- Jessie first spots Seviper in action when it is battling Ash's pal Treecko. Jessie knows immediately she wants to catch it and tries to lure Seviper with a fruit basket. It doesn't work. Instead, Jessie is able to toss her Poké Ball and seal their partnership only after Seviper chomps on her hair and eats her last rice ball.

- Seviper and Zangoose are serious rivals. Their feud is so deep, they can tell when they're in the same area and can't help but take every opportunity to fight each other. In fact, Seviper walks away from battling Pikachu just to attack Nicholai's Zangoose, over and over again. In the end, Zangoose wins, but Jessie is certainly impressed by Seviper's battle spirit!

- Although it isn't a natural competitor at Pokémon Contests at first, Seviper persists. Eventually, as part of Jessie's team, Seviper helps her get all the ribbons Jessie needs to compete in the Sinnoh Grand Festival.

YANMEGA
The Ogre Darner Pokémon

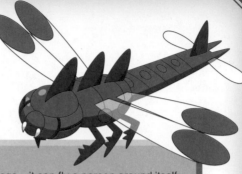

Height: 6'03"
Weight: 113.5 lbs.
Type: Bug-Flying

IMPRESSIVE SKILLS:
You don't need a plane ticket with Yanmega—it can fly a person around itself.

FUN FACTS:

- Jessie catches Yanmega when it is Yanma, but it probably won't surprise you to hear that she really stole it. Tyler, a new Trainer, is trying to catch his first Pokémon—that very same Yanma, with the help of Ash and his friends. Just as Tyler is about to toss his Poké Ball, Team Rocket swoops right in and throws theirs. So sneaky!

- Team Rocket summons Delibird to carry their Yanma catch to the Boss, but Giovanni is unimpressed with the weak Yanma and sends it back. Vain Team Rocket sees the returned Yanma as a gift. Jessie is excited to become its Trainer and immediately uses it to battle the twerps. During the battle, Yanma uses Ancient Power and evolves into Yanmega. Funnily enough, the battle is over another Yanma that Tyler and Team Rocket both want to catch. Luckily, Tyler prevails this time and Pikachu sends Team Rocket and Yanmega blasting off again.

- A blow-dryer has nothing on Yanmega's smooth Silver Wind. It makes Jessie's hair look gorgeous! It is a highlight of their performance at the Majolica Contest that helped Jessie win her second Contest Ribbon.

WOOBAT
The Bat Pokémon

Height: 1'04"
Weight: 4.6 lbs.
Type: Psychic-Flying

IMPRESSIVE SKILLS:
If you're looking to catch a Woobat, go cave searching for heart-shaped markings in the stone. Where you see hearts, there are sure to be Woobat!

FUN FACTS:
- Right as Team Rocket arrive in Unova, they call the Boss from a dark cave. Inside, a pack of Woobat flies by, and Jessie catches one! She soon uses it to battle Ash and his friends as Team Rocket tries to steal Iris's pal Axew and Ash's best friend, Pikachu. They might have been in a new region, but they're always up to their old tricks.

- At Litwick Mansion, Jessie calls on Woobat to protect her with Air Slash. It gives it its all, but Team Rocket is so desperate they even ask for help from the twerps, too—gasp!

DUSTOX
The Poison Moth Pokémon

Height: 3'11"
Weight: 69.7 lbs.
Type: Bug-Poison

IMPRESSIVE SKILLS:
When Dustox's wings flap, it sprinkles a toxic poison fleck that is so powerful it can make a pro wrestler sick.

FUN FACTS:
🔴 Jessie dreams of catching a Wurmple and helping it evolve into a Beautifly for the sole purpose of using its beauty to help her win Pokémon Contest Ribbons. Coincidentally, Ash's pal May has the same idea, and they both have their eye on the same wild Wurmple. After they get into a heated battle, Wurmple sneaks away in the hoopla. May eventually finds and catches Wurmple, only to have Team Rocket return to steal it. When May and her friends finally send Team Rocket blasting off, the trio are left hanging on to a limb over a deep canyon. But, just their luck, at the end of that limb is another wild Wurmple! Jessie tosses her Poké Ball and catches it, however, the celebration is short-lived. Wobbuffet jumps out of its Poké Ball to cheer and breaks the branch they're holding on to. While they might have a long fall down, Jessie certainly hit a career high as Wurmple's Trainer!

- From the get-go, Jessie and May have a rivalry over whose Wurmple friend is cuter. They like to talk smack and outdo each other with pampering their Pokémon pal. However, even they can't really tell the difference when they experience an accidental exchange in a Wurmple case of mistaken identity. When May goes to trade, of course, Jessie decides to keep both. Ash comes to May's aid, and Pikachu sends Team Rocket, and the right Wurmple, blasting off again!

- Both May's and Jessie's Wurmples evovle at the exact same time. Dextette reveals May's now the proud Trainer of Silcoon. Jessie thinks she, too, sees Silcoon, but her pal actually evolved into Cascoon. Meowth and James try to enlighten her, but she won't listen. While battling away with May again, it finally evolves into its final form Dustox and Jessie is forced to face the facts. Although she's confused at first, she can't help but love her darling Dustox—Jessie thinks it's cuter than May's pal Beautifly!

- Dustox helps Jessie, aka "Jessilina," win her first Contest Ribbon at the Solaceon Town Pokémon Contest. In the Performance round, they wow the audience with an explosive combination of Whirlwind and Psybeam. Ever since that day, Dustox has been wearing the ribbons Jessie wore in her hair to compete.

- Jessie and Dustox accidentally find themselves in the Dustox Crossing, a terrific time of year when there's a full moon and Dustox fall in love at a darling lake. As they couple up, they fly to Mount Coronet together and live happily ever after in pairs. Much to Jessie's surprise, her pal falls for a Dustox friend of a Trainer named Austin. Their love at first sight reminds Jessie of her first true love, one that she let go long ago. So, although Dustox is reluctant to leave Jessie, she smashes its Poké Ball to set it free to be with its Dustox partner. Jessie doesn't want her Dustox friend to make the same mistake she did, and puts its happiness first. The things we do for love!

MIMIKYU
The Disguise Pokémon

Height: 0'08"
Weight: 1.5 lbs.
Type: Ghost-Fairy

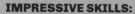

IMPRESSIVE SKILLS:
Mimikyu thinks its Pikachu rag makes it look less terrifying. And who wants to tell it the truth?

FUN FACTS:

- Team Rocket first spots Mimikyu in the forest, and it freaks them out! They are petrified of what they at first think is Pikachu's head and then realize it is a whole Pokémon in a creepy Pikachu costume. But if you ask Meowth, what it says to them is even scarier than the way it looks.

- If you've ever heard the expression "There is someone for everyone," then you won't be as surprised that Jessie finds Mimikyu cute and wants to catch it. Jessie throws Meowth into battle with it, but its Fury Swipes have no effect on Mimikyu. Worse yet, when Meowth tries to take a peek under Mimikyu's Pikachu rag, it faints and finds itself in a nightmare world. Luckily, Jessie and James are able to snap Meowth out of it by splashing it with buckets of water. For the time being, this first meeting scares off Team Rocket . . .

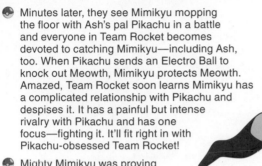

Minutes later, they see Mimikyu mopping the floor with Ash's pal Pikachu in a battle and everyone in Team Rocket becomes devoted to catching Mimikyu—including Ash, too. When Pikachu sends an Electro Ball to knock out Meowth, Mimikyu protects Meowth. Amazed, Team Rocket soon learns Mimikyu has a complicated relationship with Pikachu and despises it. It has a painful but intense rivalry with Pikachu and has one focus—fighting it. It'll fit right in with Pikachu-obsessed Team Rocket!

Mighty Mimikyu was proving very tricky to catch. When Team Rocket and Mimikyu find themselves trapped in Bewear's lair, Jessie takes the opportunity to toss her Poké Ball at Mimikyu over and over again, but Mimikyu keeps swatting it away. Then Jessie spots James's Luxury Ball and decides to steal it, much to his dismay. In a single toss, she finally catches her pal Mimikyu.

When Mimikyu's rag rips in a battle and then is stolen by Murkrow, Jessie proves her true friendship by not only recovering the rag but by stitching it back up for her Pokémon pal.

FRILLISH
The Floating Pokémon

Height: 3'11"
Weight: 72.8 lbs.
Type: Water-Ghost

IMPRESSIVE SKILLS:
Whatever you do, don't hug Frillish!
It is known to drag its prey five miles deep down into the sea.

FUN FACTS:

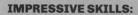

- Frillish is first introduced by Jessie in the Unova region. She calls on it in the same battle where James is first seen with his pal Amoonguss.

- Jessie's Frillish is female—but unlike with Pumpkaboo, it doesn't take a suitor for her to find out. Frillish can be both male and female, and you can tell which is which just by looking at them. Male Frillish are a bright blue, and female Frillish are a bubblegum pink.

- Team Plasma's devious doctor Colress creates a Pokémon-controlling device. When Meowth and its hilarious mind get stuck in the machine's evil clutches, Jessie calls on Frillish to rescue her talking Team Rocket Pokémon pal. Frillish's powerful Psychic floats Meowth out to freedom.

LICKITUNG
The Licking Pokémon

Height: 3'11"
Weight: 144.4 lbs.
Type: Normal

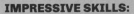

IMPRESSIVE SKILLS:
If Likitung's saliva gets on you and you don't clean it off, an intense itch will set in. The itch won't go away either.

FUN FACTS:

- While Jessie shows off some fancy snacks she purchased for the Boss, Lickitung steps out from behind some bushes and surprises them. Using its superlong tongue, it slurps up the snacks in a single lick! But its tongue doesn't stop there. It even tries to eat Jessie's new outfits. Jessie is so enraged she wants revenge. She calls on her pal Arbok to battle it, but Lickitung has it licked with a single slurp. So, Jessie thinks fast and tosses her Poké Ball to catch that Lickitung. Hey, if you can't beat 'em, join 'em!

- Jessie catches Lickitung at the perfect time, right before she competes in the Queen of the Princess Festival. In fact, Lickitung gets very close to nabbing the crown for her. With its powerful Lick, it was able to knock out Bulbasaur, Vulpix, and Pikachu! It seems Jessie and her pink pal were about to deliver a stunning win, but Misty's Psyduck seals the victory with a stunning show of Psychic power.

JAMES

Although he started out life in a very fancy family, raised in mansions and summer homes, James chose to leave it all behind to be part of Team Rocket. Now he might scrounge for food and try to steal Pokémon professionally, but he's happy! Jessie and Meowth are his constant companions, save a spat or two. And of course, between their attempts to capture Ash's pal Pikachu, James has caught many Pokémon friends of his own. In fact, James has quite a soft spot for all the Pokémon he's had the pleasure of traveling with. While the hard work of training might not be his cup of tea, he knows how to do what's best for his pals, both the Pokémon and Jessie.

MIME JR.
The Mime Pokémon

Height: 2'00"
Weight: 28.7 lbs.
Type: Psychic-Fairy

IMPRESSIVE SKILLS:
It mimics everyone it sees, but it puts extra effort into copying the graceful dance steps of Mr. Rime as practice.

FUN FACTS:

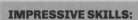

- Mime Jr. can sense emotions. So, it could tell James was sad when Chimecho was too weak to continue traveling with him. Mime Jr. saw the perfect opportunity to cheer James up with its friendship and jumped into one of his Poké Balls so it could join him.

- Mime Jr. is such a talented performer that Jessie likes to team up with it for Pokémon Contests. At the Wisteria Contest, its hula dance scores major cute points with the audience!

- James will do anything for its pal Mime Jr., including call a temporary truce with the twerps. Their peace held on just long enough for them to trade May's Egg, which had been captured by Team Rocket, for his lost pal Mime Jr.

CARNIVINE
The Bug Catcher Pokémon

Height: 4'07"

Weight: 59.5 lbs.

Type: Grass

IMPRESSIVE SKILLS:
Carnivine attracts prey with its sweet-smelling saliva, then chomps down. It takes a whole day to eat prey.

FUN FACTS:

- James is reunited with his old pal Carnivine when he visits his family's second summer cottage in Sinnoh. Carnivine had been hanging out in its Poké Ball nestled in James's beloved bottle cap collection.

- Just like Victreebel, Carnivine loves to bite James's head and has even bitten Jessie's, too! During the Jubilife Contest, Carnivine ends their entrance by taking a bite of Jessie's head. The audience thought Jessie's screaming and flailing was all part of the fun, and they finished in second place.

- During a heated battle at the Lilypad Town Pokémon Contest, Carnivine wows the crowd when it catches Mamoswine's Ice Shard. It then throws it back, and scores a direct hit and lots of applause.

WEEZING
The Poison Gas Pokémon

Height: 3'11" **Weight:** 20.9 lbs.
Type: Poison

IMPRESSIVE SKILLS:

They say two heads are better than one, but how about two bodies like Weezing? Between them, gases are mixed that can be quite toxic.

FUN FACTS:

- Every once in a while, you get a gift that changes your life. Sometimes, that gift doesn't come in a rectangular box, but rather a round Poké Ball! James gets that Poké Ball with his pal Koffing as a present for Christmas.

- Jessie often treats Weezing like it's her pal, which can bother James. She borrows Weezing to enter the Princess Festival. Then, when James and Weezing win a battle with Shellder on Seafoam Island, Jessie swoops in and catches it. The joke is on the both of them though when Shellder bites Slowpoke's tail and evolves it into a Slowbro. Then, in its evolved form, Slowbro knocks them all out and leaves. So much for stealing a new friend!

- Team Rocket likes to use Weezing's Smoke Screen to make their sneaky getaways.

GROWLITHE
The Puppy Pokémon

Height: 2'04"
Weight: 41.9 lbs.
Type: Fire

IMPRESSIVE SKILLS:
Fiercely loyal, Growlithe will do anything to protect its Trainer. It is afraid of no foe, big or small.

FUN FACTS:

- James's beloved companion from childhood, a Growlithe nicknamed Growlie, still lives with his parents. Ash assumes the biggest mansion he ever saw was where James's whole family lives, but it is really just the smaller, separate mansion for Growlie. That's one pampered Pokémon!

- Growlie is always there for James right when he needs to be protected from his mean fiancé, Jessebelle. When Jessebelle locks James up so he can't run away again, it is Growlie who busts him out. When James's treasure chest is unearthed and his marriage proposal letter to Jessebelle is found, Growlie turns it to dust with Flamethrower. What a bro!

- Although James loves Growlie, he knows his precious Puppy Pokémon will be more comfortable in its mansion than on the road with Team Rocket. James says good-bye to his old buddy and asks it to look after his parents for him.

CACNEA
The Cactus Pokémon

Height: 1'04"
Weight: 113.1 lbs.
Type: Grass

IMPRESSIVE SKILLS:
Cacnea loves to live in the dry desert. The harsher its home is, the bigger and smellier its flower crown grows.

FUN FACTS:

- James first meets Cacnea when it comes to his rescue. Team Rocket is being chased through the forest by a bunch of angry Beedrill, but before they can sting the trio, a wild Cacnea scares them all off. As thanks, James gives it a bag of treats and says good-bye, but Cacnea follows Team Rocket and asks to join them after watching them fend off a Pokémon poacher.

- Cacnea partners up with Jessie, disguised as "Jesseebella," to enter the Saffron Contest. During their performance, Cacnea scores a lot of points by hugging Jessie, but since its arms are covered in sharp thorns, Jessie is not a fan. Ouch!

- Jessie isn't the only Trainer who wants to borrow Cacnea. The Gym Leader of Eterna City, Gardenia, is obsessed with James's pal and asks if he'll lend it to her. Instead, they have a Tag Battle with Ash and Dawn, where Cacnea tries Drain Punch. Despite giving it their all, Jessie and Gardenia lose the match, but it inspires James to train Cacnea to the best of his abilities! Although James does all he can—even asking Ash for help—he feels Cacnea will be better off with Gardenia and sends his pal to train with her. Sniffle!

MORPEKO
The Two-Sided Pokémon

Height: 1'00" **Weight:** 6.6 lbs.
Type: Electric-Dark

Full Belly Mode

Hangry Mode

IMPRESSIVE SKILLS:
Morpeko is always hungry! So, it carries roasted seeds in its pouches. When it eats, it generates electricity.

FUN FACTS:

🔵 James first meets Morpeko when Team Rocket discovers the scamp eating all of their snacks. It scurries off then, but once it is hungry and back in Hangry Mode, it finds the trio again. When Team Rocket tells Morpeko it has eaten all their food, it gets so angry it blasts them off with Aura Wheel. It doesn't stay mad at its meal ticket for long though as Morpeko has been following Team Rocket ever since, even cleaning them out of food all across Galar.

🔵 Morpeko enters the Pokémon Grand Eating Contest, and it nearly wins! Its only remaining competition is Goh's pal Skwovet, but once Morpeko is full, it won't take another bite. Jessie, James, and Meowth try to get it to keep eating to win, but it blasts them off with Aura Wheel. Skowvet, on the other hand, is so determined to win that it evolves into Greedent to seal its victory! Ever since that competition, Morpeko and Greedent have had a fierce rivalry. In fact, the next time they came face-to-face, they have another eating contest, just between the two of them.

🔵 After Morpeko follows them for some time, Team Rocket feels they have turned into its personal chefs. So, they devise a plan to get the twerps to catch it, called Operation Make Them Catch Morpeko. It nearly works! Goh tries to catch it, but it is eating too furiously. In the end, the whole "operation" makes James realize he really cares for his insatiable little friend. So, he asks Morpeko to join him on his journey and officially catches it.

INKAY
The Revolving Pokémon

Height: 1'04"
Weight: 7.7 lbs.
Type: Dark-Psychic

IMPRESSIVE SKILLS:
Inkay can communicate by flashing its light spots. As they shine, Inkay spins.

FUN FACTS:

- The way to Inkay's heart is definitely through yummy food. Hungry Inkay first encounters Team Rocket when it sneakily steals James's breakfast by hiding under their table. When it tries to eat James's lunch, he cleverly tosses it both halves of a sandwich. While its arms are full, James throws a Poké Ball and catches Inkay.

- Inkay's favorite food is a flaky pastry called a croissant.

- Courageous Inkay is not afraid to pick a battle with any Pokémon, whether it's giant Pangoro or its evolved form, Malamar. In fact, it even helped to fend off three super-evil Malamar at once!

- Inkay's Psybeam is so powerful it even stops Team Flare's ray, much to Mable's dismay.

MAGIKARP
The Fish Pokémon

Height: 2'11"
Weight: 22.0 lbs.
Type: Water

IMPRESSIVE SKILLS:

Magikarp does not have any skills to speak of. It lacks strength and speed, so river currents push it around. It is considered the weakest of all Pokémon. However, it evolves into the very fierce giant Gyarados.

FUN FACTS:

- While aboard the S.S. *Anne*, James purchases Magikarp from a vendor (the same vendor he later buys a fake Chimecho from) who promises it is a gold mine. He convinces James that if he becomes a Magikarp breeder, he'll be a billionaire in no time! James gives him a whopping $300 for the Fish Pokémon and the whole kit, only to be told by his Team Rocket pals that it's the most worthless Pokémon. Wamp waaaah!

- When Team Rocket gets hungry later, they try to eat Magikarp. But it's just made of scales and bones. James becomes so angry, it kicks Magikarp out. In turn, this makes Magikarp so mad, it evolves into an enraged Gyarados that seeks revenge on its former Trainer. As Team Rocket finds out, there is no fury like a scorned Gyarados!

VICTREEBEL
The Flycatcher Pokémon

Height: 5'07"
Weight: 34.2 lbs.
Type: Grass-Poison

IMPRESSIVE SKILLS:

Victreebel lures prey with the sweet aroma of honey and then swallows it whole.

FUN FACTS:

- James's pal Weepinbell evolves into Victreebel at a fake Breeding Center run by Jessie, James, and Meowth's rivals: Butch and Cassidy. Now that it's Victreebel, it immediately does the move it is best known for—it opens its big mouth and covers James's head.

- While Ash is carrying the Indigo Plateau torch—lit by the Legendary Pokémon Moltres's flame—Meowth steals it right out of his hands. Meowth gets more than it bargained for and ends up catching on fire. James calls on Victreebel to help put his Team Rocket pal out. Of course, it covers Meowth with its big mouth, and unfortunately, they both catch on fire. Out of the goodness of Ash's heart, he asks his Water-type pal Squirtle to put them both out. Phew!

- James has been known to call his pal Victreebel "Vicky."

- When James runs into the Magikarp con man again, he asks for a refund. Instead, the con man suggests a trade—one of Team Rocket's Pokémon pals for a Weepinbell with a very sweet scent. Jessie and Meowth fall for his sales pitch and force James to trade his friend Victreebel for its pre-evolved form, Weepinbell. James is heartbroken, but when he holds their new Pokémon pal Weepinbell, he is filled with fond memories. However, their friendship doesn't last long. During their first battle with Weepinbell, it evolves into Victreebel and immediately puts Jessie in its giant mouth. New Victreebel, same old trick! When Jessie finally escapes, she is so furious, she has Arbok blast off their second Victreebel pal.

YAMASK
The Spirit Pokémon

Height: 1'08"
Weight: 3.3 lbs.
Type: Ghost

IMPRESSIVE SKILLS:

Yamask carries a mask that is said to look like it did when it was still human. It is always searching in ruins for someone who will recognize it.

FUN FACTS:

- James doesn't have to battle to catch Yamask. He notices it is hungry, offers it some food, and then asks it to join his team. Easy as pie!

- At Twist Mountain, Team Rocket calls on Yamask to try to catch a Tirtouga restored from an ancient fossil. During the heated battle, Tirtouga evolves into Carracosta. Their evil plan is foiled, though, by Ash and his friends, aka the twerps.

- Yamask has a way with Litwick. They'll do exactly what Yamask says, even if it's to try to catch Ash's pal Pikachu. Luckily, Yamask has Litwick following not-so-stellar instructions from Team Rocket, and that makes them fail in their mission, again.

- Team Rocket calls upon Yamask to help them reveal the Mythical Pokémon Meloetta. By using Will-O-Wisp, the once-invisible Pokémon is seen!

AMOONGUSS
The Mushroom Pokémon

Height: 2'00"
Weight: 23.1 lbs.
Type: Grass-Poison

IMPRESSIVE SKILLS:
Amoonguss likes to disguise itself by standing near Poké Balls that have been dropped.

FUN FACTS:

- Amoonguss is first revealed as a member of Team Rocket when James asks it to help steal Natasha's Pokémon pal Tepig.

- While trying to help Team Rocket catch their Pokémon obsession, Pikachu, Amoonguss poisons it pretty badly with its Stun Spore. Thankfully, N was on the scene and has Alomomola nurse Pikachu back to health with Refresh.

- Sometimes Stun Spore is put to good use, and James proves it! When Team Plasma is trying to control Meowth with a vicious machine Colress invented, James asks Amoonguss to use a combination of Stun Spore and Body Slam to help knock out their pal Meowth so it couldn't be used as a pawn in Team Plasma's evil plan!

MAREANIE
The Brutal Star Pokémon

Height: 1'04"
Weight: 17.6 lbs.
Type: Poison-Water

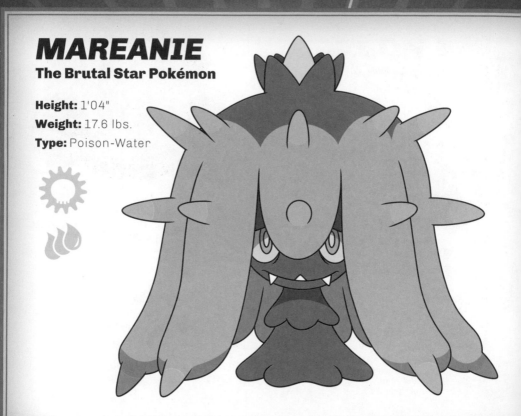

IMPRESSIVE SKILLS:

When Mareanie stings, you first succumb to being numb. Then an intense itch sets in.

FUN FACTS:

- Mareanie first falls for James because he looks like her first love, another Mareanie that's purple. But the only reason James is so purple is because Mareanie had just jumped on his head and poisoned him with Toxic Spikes. Love is strange! When James tries to run away from his lovestruck attacker, she runs after him. It is not until she helps Team Rocket nearly beat Ash and his friends in a battle that James falls for her, too. Although Bewear scoops Team Rocket up before they can celebrate a true victory, James scores when Mareanie agrees to join him on his journey.

- James is excited for the chance to try to catch Frillish, but Mareanie puts an end to that possibility. Mareanie is so jealous, it won't let James catch another female Pokémon.

- Mareanie falls for her first love when he saves her from a Tentacruel attack. However, when she later spots her hero giving another Mareanie a Corsola Horn, her heart breaks. In a chance meeting on the beach, Mareanie is reunited with her hero and first crush, but she slaps him away. The hero is so hurt he decides to attack James to win its sweet Mareanie's love back. During the fight, it evolves into terrific Toxapex. James sees this as proof of its love, but Mareanie still wants to stay with James. This makes James realize he has a Mareanie that's worth fighting for! When Toxapex attacks James with super Spike Cannon stings, he shakes it off and finally earns Toxapex's respect. Mareanie says good-bye to Toxapex for good. However, before they can part, Tentacruel attacks again and to everyone's surprise, James sends it blasting off! Mareanie and Toxapex now have a new hero.

- When Team Rocket is summoned back to headquarters, James leaves Mareanie to live happily with Mimikyu, Bewear, and Stufful in the Alola region.

CHIMECHO
The Wind Chime Pokémon

Height: 2'00"
Weight: 2.2 lbs.
Type: Psychic

IMPRESSIVE SKILLS:
On even the windiest of days, Chimecho can hang on a tree or a building by the suction cup on its head.

FUN FACTS:

- James claims it is "love at first sight" when he first spots Chimecho at a carnival as a boy. Ever since, he has always wanted to train one. However, it's such a rare Pokémon, James doesn't encounter one again for many, many years.

- It is not until the Fortree Feather Carnival, where James spots a vendor selling Chimecho—or so he thinks. Even though James realizes the vendor is same guy who gave him a bad deal on a Magikarp a long time ago, James hands over all of his money. Soon, he discovers he bought a Hoppip dressed to look like Chimecho. He was tricked again! But by some stroke of luck, a real Chimecho flies right up to James at the carnival. So, James asks it to join him, and it happily agrees! Is that the easiest catch you have ever heard of?!

- When Chimecho is too weak to continue traveling, a heartbroken James decides to put his friend's health first. He leaves it to rest with his childhood caretakers, Nanny and Pop-Pop, at his family's summer cottage.

PELIPPER
The Water Bird Pokémon

Height: 3'11"
Weight: 61.7 lbs.
Type: Water-Flying

IMPRESSIVE SKILLS:
Called the messenger of the skies, it likes to carry things like food, water, small Pokémon, and even Pokémon eggs in its big bill.

FUN FACTS:

- Pelipper delivers! All around Galar, Pelipper tracks down Team Rocket when they're in need of Pokémon partners for a battle. It drops a gadget filled with unique Team Rocket purple Poké Balls that, according to Jessie, "looks just like a gumball machine." However, instead of using coins, the gold charm on Meowth's head does the trick to score Team Rocket their temporary battle partners, which have included a terrifying Tyranitar, a powerful Poliwag, and a giant Gyarados.

- Being able to track down Team Rocket anywhere has its downside. When Scorbunny and Goh spot what they think is a wild Pelipper, they chase it in the hopes of catching it. Pelipper leads them all the way back to Team Rocket's glass phone booth and the entrance to their secret lair.

CONCLUSION

While villains aren't usually known for their softer side, Pokémon pals have certainly brought the best out of even their Team Rocket trainers. After all, that is what true friendship is about! And who can you have a deeper bond with than your awesome Pokémon friends? Through every trouble and triumph (however few), Jessie and James have their Pokémon partners to thank. They stood by them through it all, and, sure, possibly nibbled their heads or messed up their hair or accidentally poisoned them or even blasted them off sometimes, but it was all out of love for their Team Rocket buddies. Guess that's why they say close friends are "as thick as thieves"!